# SPENDING MONEY

## by Tanya Thayer

first step nonfiction

Lerner Publications Company · Minneapolis

I can **spend money.**

When I use money,
I spend it.

I spend money when
I **buy** things I want.

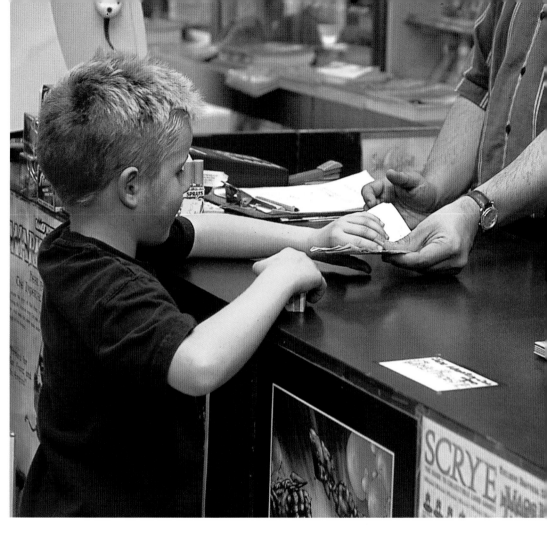

I can buy a book.

My family spends money
when we buy things we need.

I can help buy food.

I spend money when
we go somewhere.

I can go on a bus.

I spend money when
I want to have fun.

I can have a party.

I spend money when
I make a **mistake.**

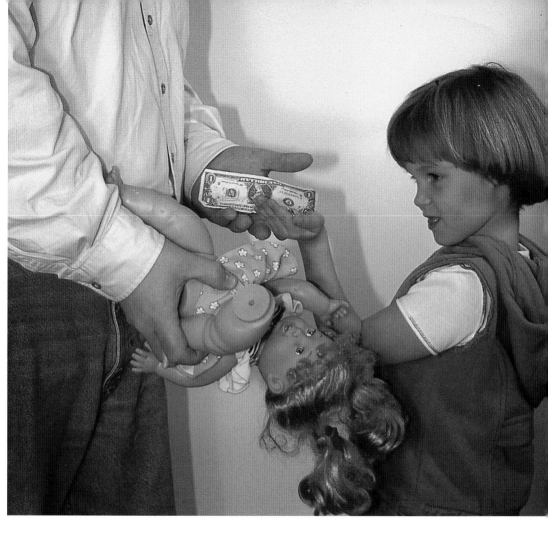

I can pay for
something I broke.

I use money when
I help others.

I can give a gift.

I can make **choices.**

I can spend money.

# Spending Pie Graph

On page 19 is a pie graph. The pie graph shows which things this child spent money on. The bigger the piece in the pie graph, the more money she spent.

What did she spend the most money on? What did she spend the least money on? What would a pie graph of the things you spend money on look like?

# I Spent Money For...

# Spending Money

 ## WHAT IS BARTERING?

Before people had paper money or coins, they would trade things to get what they wanted. For example, if you wanted your friend's red ball, you could trade your blue ball for it. But if your friend didn't want your blue ball, you would have to find something else to trade instead. This is called bartering.

## EARLY AMERICAN MONEY

When America was still a new country, coins and dollars weren't used very much. People who came to America, called colonists, used things like bullets, tobacco, and animal skins for money.

# Glossary

 **buy** – to give money for something

 **choices** – the picking of one thing from many

 **mistake** – something you do that is wrong

 **money** – what people use to buy things

 **spend** – to use money to buy things

# Index

The photographs in this book are reproduced through the courtesy of: © HMS Group/CORBIS, front cover; © Diane Meyer, 2, 22 (2nd from bottom); © D. Yeske/Visuals Unlimited, 3, 6, 9, 13, 22 (bottom); © Lynn Goldsmith/CORBIS, 4, 14; © Eric Anderson/Visuals Unlimited, 5, 16, 17, 22 (top and 2nd from top); © Michael S. Yamashita/CORBIS, 7; © Arthur R. Hill/Visuals Unlimited, 8, 10; ©Stockbyte, 11; Corbis Royalty Free Images, 12, 22 (middle); © Mark E. Gibson/Visuals Unlimited, 15; Todd Strand/IPS, 19.

Illustration on page 19 by Laura Westlund.

Lerner Publications Company
A division of Lerner Publishing Group
241 First Avenue North
Minneapolis, MN 55401 U.S.A.

Website address: www.lernerbooks.com

Library of Congress Cataloging-in-Publication Data

Thayer, Tanya.
    Spending money / by Tanya Thayer.
        p.   cm. — (First step nonfiction)
    Includes index.
    Summary: Illustrates the many ways a child can spend money.
    ISBN: 0–8225–1261–0
    1. Consumption (Economics)—Juvenile literature. 2. Children—Finance, Personal—Juvenile literature. [1. Finance, Personal.] I. Title. II. Series.
    HB820 .T43  2002
    332.024—dc21                                                      2001002445

Manufactured in the United States of America
2  3  4  5  6  7  –  DP  –  10  09  08  07  06  05